Men a
Super

Jilly Cooper's br
guide to the male sex

Jilly Cooper comes from Yorkshire and was
educated at Godolphin School in Salisbury. For
twenty-five years she lived in London and for
thirteen of them she wrote for the *Sunday Times*,
during which time her column was one of the
most widely read features in the paper. In 1982
she moved to Gloucestershire and began writing
a column for the *Mail on Sunday*. Recently she
has devoted more of her time to writing books,
ten of which have been published by Mandarin;
she is also the author of six romances, three
best-selling novels, *Riders*, *Rivals* and *Polo*, a
book of short stories, two anthologies and
several children's books. She makes frequent
appearances on television and has done many
radio broadcasts.

Jilly Cooper

Men and Super Men

with illustrations by
TIMOTHY JAQUES

Mandarin

MEN AND SUPER MEN

First published in 1972 by Eyre Methuen Ltd

This edition published in 1993
by Mandarin Paperbacks
an imprint of Reed Consumer Books Ltd
Michelin House, 81 Fulham Road, London SW3 6RB
and Auckland, Melbourne, Singapore and Toronto

Copyright © 1972 by Jilly Cooper
The author has asserted her moral rights

A CIP catalogue record for this title
is available from the British Library

ISBN 0 7493 1163 0

Printed and bound in Great Britain
by Cox & Wyman Ltd, Reading, Berks

Contents

TO GODFREY SMITH
In every way a Superman

Introduction

My only qualification for writing this book is a lifelong interest in the subject. The male—I have found—is a domestic animal which, if treated with firmness and kindness, can be trained to do most things. It is important to have one in your life to turn on your bath water, do up your zips, carry your suitcases, work out tips, tell silly jokes to, use as a threat when you are having trouble with tradesmen or unwelcome suitors and ultimately to arrange your funeral.

Men, according to legend, want only one thing, are deceivers ever, are not interested in gossip, like a cosy armful, need two eggs, and seldom wash behind their ears.

They come in all shapes and sizes except for their organs, which according to all the sex books, are exactly the same size when erect and similarly capable of giving pleasure.

At present men are under fire from the Women's Lib movement, which has been described as a storm in a B-Cup, and the biggest bore of the century, only rivalled by the Common Market. One cannot dismiss something, however, because it is boring. Every day through my letter box thunders Women's Lib propaganda: *The Feminine Mystique, Women on Women, Women under Women*, and so on.

Men in fact have come in for such a pasting that when

I started to write this book, I intended it to be in their defence—my charger and my white plume at the ready. But I found as I progressed how fundamental the antagonism between the sexes really is—how although I love a few individual supermen very deeply, as a sex men drive me up the wall. In fact if there was a third sex, I doubt if they would get a look in from me.

I find I resent the fact that I can't live without them, that they hurt me emotionally, that I hate yet secretly enjoy being bullied by them, that they can do tasks domestic far better than I can, that they enjoy the company of other men so much, and on the whole prefer a bat to a bit on the side.

My husband once went to a cricket week at his old school. I joined him for the weekend, and felt *de trop* from start to finish. I wasn't allowed to have meals with him, or even sleep in the same bed. He was in the dormitory with the rest of the team, while I was allotted one of the boys' studies (alas it was after the end of term) and had to hang my clothes on a row of male chauvinist pegs.

The second evening, bored with my own company and seething with resentment, I walked round the grounds. The air was heavy with the scent of lime trees, the black night blazed with stars. By the pavilion the two teams were having after dinner drinks. Unobserved I sat down and watched them wandering around a little unsteadily, swapping anecdotes, laughing immoderately, rolling up and down a grassy bank, scampering around in a doggy way sniffing out the most entertaining group, forming and re-forming. Away from the tension of the male-female encounter, they looked so young, handsome, carefree, and unguarded as they would never have done if there had been a woman present.

And like the Ancient Mariner, a spirit of pure love gushed from my heart, and I blessed them unaware. The self-same moment, the albatross of my resentment fell from my neck. But it was back with a vengeance as soon as I returned to my lonely truckle bed, and saw all those male chauvinist pegs again.

I have enjoyed writing this book because it enabled Tim Jaques, who did the marvellous drawings, and me to yap about sex every day on the telephone for six weeks. But when we reached the end we decided neither of us ever wanted to look at another man again.

Part 1

This is a book about men—at work and play, in bed and out of bed, in sickness and in stealth. It is also about Superman. Superman is a cross between Charles Atlas and Einstein. He keeps his figure by lifting dumb-blondes above his head before breakfast, and is sent to stud like Nijinsky at the age of twenty-one. The real hero of the book, however, is an individual called Sexual Norm.

Sexual Norm lives in the suburbs. He is married to a wife called Honor whom he has 2·8 times a week. Honor is sometimes satisfied. Norm thinks continually about other girls, but never does anything about them unless it is handed to him on a plate. He is riddled with guilt afterwards. He is doggy, pink faced, with sticking-out ears, nudging eyes, a road-up neck and a fixed avid grin. He blushes easily, laughs loudly, sweats profusely at the back of his neck, and wears dandruffy blazers.

He always has a bath in the morning—just in case—and although he has never dared enter a strip club, if a girl makes him promise not to look he usually does. He is inclined to get out of hand at office parties. His lifelong ambition is to meet a nymphomaniac.

Apart from Sexual Norm and Superman, any man a girl meets will probably fit into one or several of the following categories.

Male Types

"I'm bi-sexual—I like Sailors and Soldiers."

Soldiers have yelping laughs and very short hair, tend to have very shiny buttons on their blazers, and never talk about women in the mess. They have broad shoulders and narrow outlooks. They are straightforward and uncomplicated. Occasionally they pounce on the wives of junior officers, but the passes they are most interested in are forty-eight-hour ones. They wear mental battle dress in bed, and fatigues afterwards.

Soldiers tend to be overridden by their wives. Behind most famous soldiers you will find a very powerful dragon who has rammed her husband up the army list as a gunner might force the charge into the breech.

Sailors are always away or having it away. They have far-seeing blue eyes, and there are very few of them left now. Although they have a wife in every port, and two in Cape Town because they stop there twice, nice girls are supposed to love them. Twenty years ago they were considered very glamorous, now they are all trying to get out of the Service and failing to make it in Industry.

Sailors are always rabbiting on about their fine tradition, which as Churchill claimed consisted of nothing but Rum, Sodomy and the Lash.

There is absolutely nothing I can think of to say about Airmen at all.

SCIENTISTS

Scientists have the shortest hair and the thickest spectacles. They wear white coats, talk in whispers, and have never read a book. When they meet a pretty girl they turn pink like litmus paper and have difficulty raising a retort stand. They are all described as brilliant to compensate for being on the non-smart side of the two cultures, and tend to be left wing.

They have a curiously cold analytical approach to women, and are too busy making explosions to have much fire in their bellies.

They are the first target for Rats' Lib.

THE CLERGY

"For what we are about to receive . . ."

In theory the clergy don't—except with their wives or the bishop if he asks them. In fact it is difficult for them to get off with anyone, as unlike catholic priests they don't have the intimacy of the confessional. It must also be a bit turning off to have a whole pewful of parish hats gazing at you with adoration every Sunday.

Perhaps they say: "For who we are about to receive may the Lord make us truly thankful," before they pounce on you, and then send you to the jumble sale afterwards. They are all tone deaf.

DOCTORS

Very easy to get at. Anyone can pretend to have a migraine or pains in the chest. But the Hippocratic oath stops doctors doing anything about it, unless you meet them at a cocktail party or down in the shopping centre. I think most women imagine that because doctors know so much about the female body, they'll be better at making love to it. I should hate to have it off with a doctor in case he found some bump or cavity he shouldn't.

LORRY DRIVERS

Available to hitch-hikers. They make love at 20 miles an hour and have red lights on their rears. They spend a lot of time in lay-bys. A girl friend of mine had a fantasy about lorry drivers in which she passed them a note saying: "You can come home with me as long as you don't speak."

STOCKBROKERS

Stockbrokers play squash all the time—they squash

themselves against women all the way to the City on the Tube, then play squash in the evening to keep their weight down. Later in the evening they play bridge, or go to cocktail parties and shout at girls with flicked up hair and bare foreheads. During the day they make up filthy stories and think about Bulls and Bears.

At weekends they make desperate attempts to be trendy, tripping off to the launderette in sweaters, paisley scarves flowing through a brass ring, their trousers held up under a spreading stomach by a stockbroker belt.

There are very few pretty girls working in the City, which is one of the places to go to if you want to hook a man.

THE LEGAL PROFESSION

Most women, being irrational, will be driven up the wall by the pedantic exactitude of the legal mind. Occasionally a lawyer sends you a legal document covered in kisses, and you really think you're getting somewhere until he tells you he only wants you to sign your name, in three places. And his indecent proposal will be couched in such convoluted jargon, you won't have a hope of defending your honour against him. He will overrule all your objections.

On the whole, barristers are more interested in their briefs than yours. They tend to be pompous and divide you mentally into twelve good men and true when they talk to you. They also put their upper lips in rollers every night, so they can sneer better at their opponents.

TELEVISION (See Fairies)

Men in television brush their hair forwards, and wear white polo-necked sweaters, suede jackets, name-tag bracelets, and deaf aids. They spend their time gossiping—the television centre in Wood Lane is built in a circle to enable the gossip to travel more quickly—and in backbiting—you can recognise a television man once he takes his clothes off because his shoulders are covered in stab marks.

POLITICIANS

Vote Libertine.

Politicians have ringing voices, graciously waving hands, and an all-embracing smile that passes over you like a lighthouse beam. They also make love on all three channels.

Like most men in power they have a hayride sexually—all women wanting to go to bed with a 20,000 majority.

Because on the whole they work so hard, politicians become tremendously randy on the rare times they are off-duty, and because the newspapers are always saying nasty things about them and thwacking them on their marginal seats, they need the reassurance of sexual conquest to soothe their bruised egos. It is very easy for them to be unfaithful because once they're in the House they become completely ungetatable, and their wives never know if they're snoozing on a back bench, chairing a committee meeting or carrying on an affaire of state.

Women, being naturally subservient, are generally

attracted to a man in a position of authority—whether he's a doctor, a psychiatrist, a solicitor who advises them when they're in trouble, a general in time of war, a teacher at night school, a ski instructor, or most often their boss.

SCHOOLMASTERS

Going for a Thong

Schoolmasters however are a very different cup of tea— 'children among men, men among children', as Dr Johnson called them. They have chalk in their hair, are dry as dust, hearty, antiseptic, and almost invariably undersexed. They adore the sound of their own voices, and often develop tics and private jokes. Ill at ease in the company of women, they prefer the adulation of a captive audience, their pupils, or the fusty misogyny of their colleagues.

Being accustomed to school dinners, they invariably take girls to awful restaurants. Naturally bossy, they treat their wives like little boys of eleven.

Recommended for masochistic ladies—they are very good at knocking the stuffing out of those smaller than themselves.

FARMERS

Farmers have red faces, purple raw hands and straw in their turnups. They wear long jackets, frequently suffer from calf love, and wear gumboots to keep the sheep steady. They get up very early in the morning and assist in the sexual couplings of animals. In summer they get bitten by insects, and summon milkmaids and landgirls to

"But I have taken them off, darling."

come and see their itchings. Their houses smell of pigs.

Gentlemen farmers spend their time drinking at lunchtime, butchering wildlife, riding in point-to-points and swapping wives. At hunt balls, one glass of bubbly turns them as scarlet as their coats, and soon every cordoned off fourposter is heaving with occupants.

ACTORS

Actors, unlike farmers, get up very late, and go to bed after midnight, unless they are getting up at the crack of dawn to play in some film. As a race, they're inclined to be surprisingly insecure, self-obsessed, only interested in talking shop, and finding out whether Quentin was perfectly frightful at Bristol.

Actors like to make love in front of a looking glass so they can admire their own performance, or with the television on, so they can see how 'perfectly frightfully' all their friends are acting. If they keep their socks on, they're either a blue movie star or terrified of getting foot rot.

On the credit side, they are marvellous at playing out one's fantasies, whether you want them to dress up as a sadistic schoolmaster, a vicar, or a gentleman farmer.

MUSICIANS

Musicians dress very badly, sometimes suffer from Hallé Orchestra and enjoy playing the eternal triangle. Singers however have the most marvellous breath control and can kiss for at least ten minutes without stopping. Trumpeters and any player of woodwind instruments are also very good at kissing, having such mobile lips. Violinists have very versatile left hands—I really dig that double stopping.

Conductors have superb timing: anyone who conducts a whole orchestra shouldn't have much trouble conducting an affaire.

If a man keeps boasting: "Look no hands," while making love to you, he's probably a concert pianist or a brain surgeon and frightened of losing his no-claim bonus.

WRITERS

Writers are alleged to write about it better than do it. Certainly they always regard you as copy, and if you make a *bon mot* while they're making love to you, they'll leap off you and rush away to find a pen and write it down.

However, it is nice to get sonnets from time to time. They also write wonderful letters, which are absolute hell to answer, not much about oneself and full of all those fragments from Donne and Marvell.

One writer I know has an unnerving habit of taking two extra copies of all his love letters, one for himself, the other for the British Museum.

PAINTERS

Painters dress well, and have very nice handwriting. But don't be fooled by that line about only seeing you as a beautiful form not as a sexual object. It's the easiest way I know to get a woman to remove her clothes.

I think on the whole those involved in the arts make the best lovers, for they have more imagination, more ability to cater for your fantasies, and a bigger repertoire. Most of them have a kind of feline, slightly feminine mind—pure heaven from start to fetish. But don't expect fidelity. Art has very little to do with morals.

ADVERTISING MEN

Most of their time is spent making presentations or discussing whether they should insert their eight-inch single column more than three times a week. They dress very well, if somewhat uniformly—navy blue suit, pink shirt—and are generally doused in free sample scent. When you meet them at parties, they say: "Actually I'm in advertising," in a very apologetic way, because *au fond* they feel they ought to get out and do something worthwhile like writing unprofitably, or painting unsellably. Nearly all of them have unsold novels in their bottom drawers and most of them live in Fulham. They have hearts with natural breaks in them.

Stages of Man

Now leaving the professions we move on to some of the stages of man.

YOUTHS (See Schoolboys or Students)

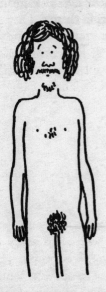

"But of course there's nothing wrong with you, Adrian darling—I just can't stand red hair . . ."

In my youth, youths used to breathe heavily, say thank you three times if you gave them a cigarette, open the matchbox upside down so that the matches cascaded onto the floor, and finally knock over the ashtray.

Today youths are extremely cool, have lean and hungry pelvises and hip measurements in single figures. They often marry at seventeen and refer to their father-in-law as 'baby'. They don't talk if they don't feel like it, but this is probably because in the places they frequent, the music is so loud as to make conversation impossible. They wear clothes which disconcert their elders, including tight jeans to emphasise a bulging crotch. They spend most of their time strumming on guitars or trendy-looking girls who look as though they've just crawled out from underneath a rolling stone. Secretly these girls will worry about tight jeans making a man impotent.

STUDENTS (See Airmen)

OLDER MEN

Peter Pan and Trendy.

It has always seemed unfair to me that no one bats an eyelid if a man goes out with a girl thirty years younger than he is, but everyone starts prophesying doom and desertion if a woman shacks up with a man even three years younger than herself. A woman left by her husband when she is forty either faces living alone or has to break up someone else's marriage if she's going to get married again, whereas a forty-year-old divorced man can have a ball with any dolly he chooses.

As a result the world is now full of seventy-year-old ravers, locks clustering over the collars of their shirts, sideboards laddering their artificially tanned cheeks, and fifty-year-old ton-up boys, forcing themselves into tight jeans, brushing their thinning hair forward, and touching up the grey roots of their jet-black Viva Zapata moustaches. In the evening they wear sawn-off kaftans to hide their pot bellies.

In an attempt to keep up, they exhaust themselves going on vegetarian diets, giving up drink, and dancing all night in discothèques, then going round with grey faces saying they feel twenty years younger. In trying to be Peter Pan, they look more like petered-out pansies.

They also embrace all the phoney mysticism that surrounds smoking pot, and at parties they can be seen going furtively into back rooms and tearing cigarettes apart. Later they gaze into young girls' eyes and say: "My dear, you've made an old man very hippy."

Dolly birds like them—because it gives them kudos in the typing pool to be going out with an older man. Older men can also take them to trendy restaurants younger men can't afford, and are said to be 'experienced' sexually. (I shudder to think what rubbish is dished up in the name of experience.) They also take them occasionally for dirty weekends at a Truss House in Hernia Bay.

FIANCÉS

Fiancés are out of date and not getting it. If pressed they will say: "My fiancée and I have slept together all night in

"Oh for heaven's sake, Harriet ..."

the same bed, but we haven't actually slept together."
Fiancées never give their fiancés their all—only about
seven-eighths.

Fiancés have soft curly hair, pink faces from permanently blushing at their predicament, starry eyes, and a
mosaic of scarlet lipstick on their downy cheeks from
having been embraced by so many new aunts-in-law.

They also manage to appear vacant and engaged at the
same time by having a far away abstracted expression on
their faces. People naturally assume they are dreaming of
the moment when they and their betrothed will be one
flesh; actually they are completely shell-shocked by all the
talk about soft furnishing and wedding-present lists.

Caught off guard, they have a trapped expression.

As one fiancé said, just before his wedding: "I feel as though I'm going into hospital for a major operation and all the anaesthetists are on strike."

On their desks they have photographs of their fiancées given them by their fiancées, looking mistily soppy in pearls.

BACHELORS

Bachelors begin at thirty-six. Up till this age they are regarded as single men. Most of them are very tidy, smell of mothballs, and have an obsessional old maid's fix about one of their ashtrays being moved an inch to the right. Because they are not married, or living with a woman, they don't feel the need to bath very often. Occasionally they have a shower after cricket and pinch their married friends' towels. They can be recognised by their white underpants. (Married men have pale blue or pink-streaked underpants, because one of their wife's scarves has run in the washing machine.)

Bachelors dread Christmas because they've got so many god-children to remember, and have a very high threshold of boredom through enduring so many grisly evenings with awful girls thrust on them by their married friends.

By way of revenge, they spend a great deal of time sponging off their married friends, turning up for lunch on Sunday and not leaving until the Epilogue, and knocking their disgusting pipes out on the carpet so that they get a chance to look up the wife's skirt when she bends over to sweep up the mess.

They also get wildly irritated by their friends' children, cast venomous glances at a two–year–old, and say: "Isn't it time he went to prep school?"

A married man often rings up his bachelor friend and after a lot of humming and hawing asks if he can borrow the flat to 'change in' that afternoon. When the bachelor gets home in the evening, he often finds various bits of female underclothing, and his bed has been far more tidily made than he left it that morning.

Married friends are also inclined to turn up with whisky bottles, having been locked out by their wives, and spend all night berating the matrimonial state.

It is hardly surprising that although a lot of bachelors

"So *pleased* to beat you . . ."

would like to get married, they cannot bring themselves to take the plunge—like bathing on Christmas Day.

Bachelors can mostly be divided into the following categories:

GAY BACHELORS (See Fairies and Airmen)

ELIGIBLE BACHELORS

They have three address books, and an ejector seat for getting girls out of their flats in the morning. They never have any free evenings because they are constantly being asked out to dinner by designing mums or married women for their divorced girl friends.

MOTHER'S BOYS

"Darling, this is Mummy ..."

They wear scarves, berets, long macintoshes, galoshes and often work for the White Fish Authority. They always wash apples before they eat them and suffer from hypochondria. When they say they have relations all the time, they don't mean sexual ones, only that they live at home with their mother and sisters.

They have hot milk with skin on it before they go to bed, and read the Lesson on Sunday. People often say they need the love of a good woman, but what they need is the love of a really bad woman to get them off the hook.

They wear camel-hair dressing gowns and grey striped pyjamas. Penalty for pulling the cord is disillusionment.

MARRIED MEN

Let's Play Monogamy.

Married men mostly chat up girls to bolster their self-respect and prove they haven't lost their touch. They are more likely to flash photographs of their children at you than anything else. Although they may claim they're unhappily married and carry on something shocking at parties, they seldom leave their wives for other men.

The confirmed adulterer usually operates from a position of strength: "I'm very much in love with Jennifer, you know. I wouldn't do anything to endanger my marriage, and little Gideon and Samantha mean everything to me."

When you ask if his wife ever gets up to tricks, knowing from the gripevine that she does, he shakes his head smugly and says: "Oh no, Jennifer never looks at another man." (Presumably she does it with her eyes shut.)

I think married people should only have affaires with other married people who know the rules (a sort of: "If you don't leave scratch marks on my back, I won't leave scratch marks on yours"), keep the same hours and are batting from the same position of strength and weakness. There is a freemasonry about married people: they seem to feel it doesn't matter how much they hurt the single person they got entangled with, as long as nothing is allowed to endanger the married state.

But as with older men, it gives a girl terrific kudos in the typing pool to say she's having an affaire with a married man—everyone imagines he looks like Mr Rochester. And the hours are good too. She'll have most evenings and all weekends free, including Easter and Christmas, to run another man.

Younger married men often have their trousers done up with a nappy pin, and black rings under their eyes, not from making love all night but from teething babies. Wedding rings are worn by men who marry foreign girls or who think other people might think they were not attractive enough to get anyone.

Married men of course vary enormously. Some are so henpecked they're absolutely covered in beak-marks, and a burglar alarm goes off if another woman so much as shakes hands with them. Others have what are called adultery toleration pacts, which means they can go off and sleep with whom they like, as long as they tell their wives all about it afterwards. It is all a question of wife-styles.

DIVORCED MEN

"I'm not so old and not so plain, and I'm quite prepared to marry again."
                                                         W. S. GILBERT.

It always amazes me how vitriolic divorced people are to each other. One girl friend of mine came back from work to find her drawing room piled high with dusty books. Her ex-husband had arrived and taken all the book-shelves away because he'd put them up in the first place.

Another wife stripped her house of all its possessions and moved in with her lover. Three days later there was a knock on the door: it was a special delivery of 400 gallons of water.

"But I didn't order any water," she protested.

"This was the address we were given," said the delivery man, handing her a note. It was from her husband, saying: "You forgot to take the water out of the swimming pool."

Divorced men can be divided into two types: those who left their wives, and those that were left by their wives. If you marry the former, you worry that he's going to do the same to you, if you marry the latter, you worry whether he's still crazy about his first wife, and trying to compete with her. First wives always look like Scarlett O'Hara, or are wonderful little homemakers like Katie in the Ads, who spend their time running up thousands of delicious puddings tasting of Oxo. Or they are boots who don't get married again and cost their husbands a fortune in alimony.

Even if a man's first wife doesn't cast a long shadow, there are always his children to amuse on those eternally long weekends. Scenting weakness, they generally play the

"I got it from a 13th century recipe. Was it all right?"

new wife up shamelessly. If she cooks their favourite food, they say their mother makes it much better. If she plays with them, they get over-excited and won't go to bed. If she tries to suck up to them and buy them expensive presents, they've always got them already.

And then there are those endless dreary afternoons on the Serpentine steering the little mites away from necking couples, or at the Zoo steering them away from copulating animals.

If she's a girl friend rather than a wife, they spend their time telling her how much prettier the girl friend was who came last weekend. Having snapped at them, she remembers they're victims of a broken home and feels guilty.

"Now, come on children, you do remember Susan . . ."

Don't catch men on the rebound immediately after they've been left by their wives: they'll sob all over you, and then go off with someone else.

Any girl who is determined to get married should go for a man who's been married six times, and get him into bed. He will then divorce his sixth wife and marry her, being one of those incurable romantics who believes that if he sleeps with a girl he's got to do the decent thing by her.

Divorced men who show no sign of marrying again and appear to be thoroughly enjoying themselves will be a constant source of irritation to their friends, for the men will be jealous and the wives will sense their husbands' jealousy.

Another person who will be disapproved of by society if he appears to be enjoying himself is the lover.

"There always seems something so dirty-sweatered and dirndl-skirted about living with a man you're not married to."

ELAINE DUNDY

Lovers live in unmarried respectability, furnish their love-nests from Co-habitat, and are disapproved of by society, which feels that the man is having his cake and eating it and that both of them shouldn't be avoiding tax. Society is slightly less shocked by men living in sin with girls under twenty-four, because it doesn't feel the man has yet ruined the girl's chances of getting married.

It never enters anyone's head that it might be the girl who is refusing to get married.

Lovers in fact behave far more respectably than married couples. Have you ever heard of a mistress-swapping party? Although they wear their unconventionality in public like a banner, in private they are watching television, washing up and having sex 2·8 times a week like everyone else.

A liaison like this usually begins when a girl is moving flats and wants to leave her luggage somewhere so she dumps it with her boy friend. Before he really knows it, she's moved in, had a key cut, changed the wallpaper in the drawing room, and is adding the usual little feminine touches—bras dripping over the bath, make-up on the carpet. For the first few months they enjoy the thrill of living in sin and playing at being married. The possibility that Daddy might roll up with a horse-whip adds an edge to the situation. Soon other couples are asking them to dinner and they start asking them back, until it becomes a habit.

Men who are living with women are at pains to tell you within five minutes that they are not actually married. On the whole they seem to be more overtly randy than married men just to prove they're not tied down.

SCHOOLBOYS (see Students, Bachelors, Lovers, Married Men, Divorcés)

Class

Class as a subject is as taboo today as sex was during Victorian times. Nevertheless there are still certain differences between the classes.

THE ARISTOCRACY

  Sir Galahad everyone in sight

"Open yer legs, dam' yer!"

Aristocrats spend their childhood being beaten by fierce nannies and their later years murdering wildlife, so it's hardly surprising their sex lives are a bit cock-eyed. When they get 'awf' with a girl they automatically expect her to go to bed with them—a hangover, I suppose from the old *droit de seigneur* days. The girl will have to experience a good many *gaucheries de seigneur* first, including a lot of coarse fishing around to find where her bra unclasps. She should be careful if she makes love to him in his own house, or the bedroom door may be suddenly flung open and the general public pour in, having been charged 50p to see over her.

Aristocrats have their mouths permanently open so that the back of their throats is coated with flies like a windscreen after a long journey. They have double-barrelled fowling pieces, wives called Fiona, and never *go* on holiday.

THE MIDDLE CLASSES

The middle class man indulges in wife-swapping parties and swinging—it is all-important for him to keep it up in front of the Joneses. He buys a great many porny books and magazines which he carefully locks away every morning, in case the daily woman finds them. He inconsistently disapproves of what he calls P.D.A.—public displays of affection, or necking in the street. The words 'privacy of one's own home' are often on his lips. He keeps a large box of Kleenex for Men by the bed.

THE LOWER CLASSES

Ever since *Lady Chatterley's Lover*, the lower classes have retained a tremendous reputation for being sensation in the sack—more vigorous and muscular, less fastidious. It's all part of the New Brutality.

Photographers of both the lower and the upper classes are very much in vogue. But the upper class ones have to say 'yer know' every five minutes, and 'ubsolutely funtustic', to show how democratic they are. Photographers have long arms like monkeys from carrying so much equipment about, and usually shack up with models so they can talk shop in bed instead of doing anything else. And they don't have to pay any model fees.

SNOBS

"I came up the hard way. The lift wasn't working."

Snobs or parvenus are very much to be avoided as it's chips on the shoulder with everything. To justify his own insecurity, the snob tries to pull any girl he meets, a case of local boy makes everyone.

His intentions are always honourable: unless you have a title, he will never marry you. What are a few nights of passion to him compared with a lifetime at the wrong end of the table.

I once went out with a Harrovian parvenu. He said: "I fancy you more than any woman I've ever met, but I can't marry you because you're not Upper Class Enough."

I was later irritated to see his smug little face in the Tatler on his wedding day, a horse-faced duchess's daughter on his arm flanked by a battalion of large bridesmaids. Tiara Boom-de-ay. Many parvenus are:

RICH MEN

"His voice was full of money."   DOROTHY PARKER.

Rich men are much more attractive than poor men,

beggar men or thieves, but not all that interested in sex. They're too busy training camels to jump through the eye of a needle, and worrying about being down to their last villa in the South of France.

Rich men come complete with all mod cons, saunas, swimming baths, indoor and outdoor barbecues and flagellation rooms. They are marvellous between the balance sheets.

They are funny about money, suspicious of being used, and afraid they are not being loved for themselves alone and all that.

It would be very boring to marry a really rich man, for he'd either be at the office night and day, or else under your feet all the time. You'd spend your life playing tinker tailor with the caviare, and waiting for Jackie Onassis to ask you to coffee parties.

Sexual Types

NARCISSISTS

One of the great misconceptions is that women don't like very good-looking men. They do—the best lovers are either men who cater for and play on your fantasies or who are so beautiful you don't need to fantasise at all. The trouble is that beautiful men aren't usually interested in women.

You also have to spend so much time jostling with them for the mirror, telling them how marvellous they look, and knowing they're only gazing passionately into your eyes to admire their reflection in your dark glasses. And because they feel secure on the basis of their looks, they're inclined to be apathetic in bed.

They are also a bit boring about keeping fit, not eating or drinking much and getting up early to do press-ups. The only press-ups a man ought to do should be on one.

They usually have portraits of themselves in the attic getting older and older, and marry plain women because they don't like competition.

FAIRIES

Every girl should have one at the bottom of her.

One is inundated with so much improperganda these

days that it's easy to think everyone is queer. You can be quite sure, though, if a young man comes floating up to you with flowing locks, gaudy shirt, matching flowered tie, a mass of necklaces, rings on each finger like a knuckle-duster, bells on his toes, clouds of scent, and says "Hullo Baby" in a soft gentle voice, that he's not queer.

Everyone thinks all actors are queer. That's why the straight ones rush round making it with women to prove they're not. I always wonder what the gay ones think when they have to kiss girls on stage: "Shut your eyes, and think of Equity," I suppose.

People automatically assume that hairdressers and antique dealers are queer, but this is no longer so. Since both professions became big business, the butch has moved in.

THE LOUSE BEAUTIFUL

The toast is absent fiends.

Lice Beautiful have accounts at the sex shop, seen-it-all-before eyes, and a million light years of sexual experience under their belts. They also smell of sulphur and brimstone rather than aftershave.

The bounder will love you and leave you, but he'll never put a tongue wrong while he's loving you. If he stuck around you'd find he'd got hidden shallows, that he is the kind of man who has to keep on making love to women because he can't think of anything to say to them in between.

"I'll definitely see you before the weekend, or after the

weekend," he says as he whisks off in his Lotus Elan after a night of passion. Next morning he'll send you two dozen red herrings.

He seldom likes other men, his philosophy being like Byron's, a compound of misanthropy and voluptuousness.

"Hate thy neighbour and love thy neighbour's wife."

TOUCHERS

Excellent well, thou art a fleshmonger.

Touchers cannot keep their hands off you, they must touch flesh and are not safe in taxis. If they're not pinching your bottom, they're propelling you across the road, or putting their hands round your waist six inches too high. If you remonstrate with them they give you a lecture on the importance of grope therapy, and you end up feeling you're both frigid and riddled with inhibitions.

GIGOLOS

Gigolos have the sort of hair styles that make older men snort, pencil in their moustaches every morning and cruise around with For Hire signs on their foreheads. They walk with bent knees because they're so weighed down with presents, gold rings, cufflinks, watches, necklaces, and stoppings.

CASANOVA—the Great Lover.

I've always wondered why Casanova himself was so

"Harry—for God's sake not now!"

successful. It must be something to do with stamina: anyone who can keep up a diary let alone anything else for twelve volumes, must have remarkable staying power. Another secret of their success is blanket coverage. They ask every woman they meet to go to bed with them, and though they get their faces slapped fairly often, they also notch up some conspicuous victories. Others concentrate on ugly girls. Nostalgie de la boot, I suppose.

But how many women do you chalk up before you become a Casanova? My husband says 43, which sounds a somewhat arbitrary figure, but he refuses to elucidate. He believes Casanova provides a useful social service, claiming that the best women, like Rolls-Royces, should be delivered to the customer fully run in.

Reputation helps, of course. Once a man has established himself as Mr Rat, women can't wait for him to come along, for they see themselves as the saviour who halts the Rake's Progress. Or as one libertine said of his ex-wife: "She complained I was too well endowed and went on too long, a remark which did me no disservice with her friends."

But what motive drives the compulsive womaniser on to fresher and fresher feels? Like the sportsman who sees a duck flying across the sky and can't resist taking a pot at it, some men have bigger sexual appetites, I suppose, or are frightened of commitment and find safety in little numbers.

The difference between Casanovas and the Louse Beautiful type is that Casanovas like women and enjoy making love to them. "I love the sex," they cry, like Macheath. "Nothing unbends the mind like them."

Whereas Lice Beautiful only take pleasure in conquest. They regard women like Kleenex tissues, to be cast aside once they've been used, or like the pilot who, as the 109th Messerschmitt plunges flaming to the ground, leans calmly out of the cockpit and chalks another swastika on his fuselage.

Some men are promiscuous because they're unhappy, or frightened of growing old and losing their pulling power; others like the brinkmanship of living dangerously.

But promiscuity feeds upon itself. If two women in a man's life are cross with him because he's not giving them enough attention, he invariably moves off in search of approbation and a clean slate, which sets up a chain reaction. Nobody too arouses more disapproval tinged with envy among other men than a Casanova. Empty pots, they mutter darkly, latent homosexual, only doing it because he hates women. No wonder Casanovas get a bit twitchy about their images.

"I'm not promiscuous," said one outraged libertine. "I just like girls."

VOYEURS

Beautiful people looking through beautiful peep-holes.

Part 2

Action

FANCYING

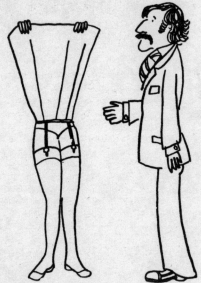

*"Tom—do come and meet Cynthia—she's been dying
to meet you for ages."*

*"To think I have wasted years and years of my life, that
I have longed for death, that the greatest love I have ever
known is for a woman who doesn't please me."*

MARCEL PROUST.

I have always contended there are two kinds of fancying.
Some men you hardly notice for weeks, and then the whole
thing jells like mayonnaise. Others you meet—and it's lust
at first sight. But the libido is so irrational. The quality you
dote on in one man, you put up with a total lack of in

another. Men are just the same.

"I'm a tit man, I'm a leg man, I'm a behinds superman," they cry, and promptly fall for quite the opposite. Ever since I was three, boys have been sidling up to me and saying: "I like my women subtle, but I'm making an exception in your case."
Or:
"My wife likes tailored costumes. I can't really think why I fancy you." Then they quote Herrick's 'Sweet disorder in the dress', and feel better.

And people are always saying: what *does* he see in her? Probably no more initially than a favourable reflection of himself in the girl's eyes. Sexual Norm fancies anyone who shows a glimmer of interest in him. Superman is invariably drawn to some cool ice-maiden, because he wants to ruffle her plumage—it's all part of the untrodden snow syndrome.

I think it's mostly a question of chemistry. People either click sexually or they don't, and if they don't, well, nothing will make a magnet attract a silver churn.

The libido also likes to do its own hunting. That's why blind dates or 'awfully sweet' men people fix you up with seldom work out. I can understand exactly why Chi-Chi and An-An never got off the ground.

Then of course there's the 'Snob'. Proust has a theory that people, particularly women, fall in love in the direction they want to go socially, which is why M.P.s, aristocrats, generals in time of war, and even Prime Ministers and of course dustmen, clean up. The most indolent women have been seen running to catch a boss.

I really fancied an actor I met at a party the other day, but was appalled to find myself rapidly losing interest when someone told me he never got any work. And while we're on the subject of actors, the libido never fails to surprise. Australian women recently voted Peter Wyngarde the man they most wanted to lose their virginity to. Men with big feet are fancied because they are reputed to be well endowed elsewhere.

When a man says a woman isn't his type, it's a polite way of saying he thinks she's totally sexless—but when people say a man has frightful taste in women, it means he's having a ball with girls his friends rigidly disapprove of. Some unfortunate masochists only fancy women who give them a hard time. As Shaw grumbled: "The fickleness of the women I love is only equalled by the infernal constancy of the women who love me."

In fact so much misery is caused by people falling in love with people who don't fall for them, or marrying totally unsuitable people merely because they momentarily fancied them enough to propose, that one cannot help feeling the whole thing is some monstrous legpull, that the Gods are laughing themselves sick up in the skies.

HOW TO MEET MEN

One of the basic dissatisfactions of a girl's life is walking round and round the streets, seeing the most heavenly men wandering about and not being able to get at them. There is not much consolation in the fact that if you met them they might be as boring as hell.

But where do you find men? Oxford and Cambridge

used to provide inexhaustible supplies in the Old Days. One had only to learn to type there, or land a job in one of the colleges, or if you were brainy go to one of the women's colleges, to have a string of men chasing after you. But since National Service was abolished, I am told all the male undergraduates are 'too amazingly young to be any good to anyone'.

There are also more men in the country—because they have to stay where their jobs are—whereas all the girls head straight for London believing this is where the action is. As it is, girls outnumber the men there by about six to one. Most of them end up as secretaries to boring married men, and spend their evenings gazing at the wallpaper in their bedsitters.

You are also supposed to meet men at parties, but how do you get asked to parties if you don't know anyone? Then of course there's evening classes and meaningful glances across the basketwork or the thrown pot—or joining a club, which gives one awful visions of Youth Clubs full of scoutmasters or eager beavers called Stanley with badges on their lapels—or computer dating, which doesn't seem to work much because you can't computerise chemistry and everyone lies like hell. If someone asks you if you consider yourself utterly irresistible, quite irresistible, resistible, or canned nightmare, you are hardly likely to put canned nightmare.

Picking up men in the street or in restaurants is dodgy because you never know if you've landed the Boston Strangler, and there's always the irrational feeling that if he's got time to go round picking up girls he must be desperate, even though you're doing exactly the same thing yourself.

On the other hand it's different picking up men on aeroplanes (on the false assumption that if he can afford a plane ticket he must be rich), on holiday (the same applies) and at art galleries or at concerts (if he loves beauty he can't be all bad). The Tate Gallery incidentally at week-ends is one of the best pick-up places in London.

I have also been reading *The Sensuous Man*, which encourages men who want to meet women to hunt them out in the supermarket. Instead of pinching a pretty woman's bottom, a man pinches her trolley 'by mistake' and whisks it down to the check counter. When she rushes shrieking after him, he offers to pay for her groceries, and this way strikes up a friendship. So next time you're in the supermarket, and you see a man lurking, throw a few jars of caviare and peaches in brandy into your wire basket.

Another method the book recommends is for the man to bump into a girl in the High Street and send her parcels flying. He then picks them up, gets into conversation, and offers to buy her a drink to make up for any bruises or breakages he may have inflicted. (This ploy can, pre-sumably, only be used in licensing hours.) It strikes me as being rather extreme—one has visions of the pavements of Oxford Street getting as bad as the M1 in a fog. Perhaps they'll install a Pederasts Crossing for men who don't want to get caught up in the rough and tumble.

THE CHAT UP

"Oh, you say that to all the girls."   DICK EMERY SHOW.

Well, he does fancy you and he's decided to do something about it, so he starts chatting you up. You notice the preliminary switching on of casualness, the quick range-estimating glance, the perceptible inner girding of loins, or squaring of shoulders. Sexual Norm straightens his Club tie, smooths his sweater down over his bottom, pulls in his stomach, whips off his spectacles, crinkles his eyes engagingly, and puts on his goat *fatale* face. He then goes upstairs, brushes his hair, and starts all over again.

"Please, Mr Elmhurst, put me down this instant!"

Usually a man indicates his interest in you by shooting you a penetrating glance, which you return and hold just a second longer than is polite, as you say: "Whoops tra la, here we go again." Soon your eyes are meeting so often in penetrating glances it doesn't matter that you've got nothing to say or he's talking about garden sheds.

Superman, when he's chatting you up, never lets his eyes swivel to see if there's something more amusing behind you, he howls with laughter at your weakest joke, and remembers what you've said an hour later.

He only leaves your side, even if he's given every chance of escaping, to go and fetch you another drink, so he can shoot you a long-distance smoulder across a crowded room, then bolt back to your side again. He keeps telling you how pretty you are, which works a treat—all women like a bit of buttering-up with their bed. Occasionally he touches your hand when he lights your cigarette. Sexual Norm, in an attempt at sophistication, puts the cigarette in his own mouth to light it for you, and hands it to you all soggy.

A lot of men chat up girls by being rude to them. But personally I don't fancy the plain blunt type. If a man's likely to put me down, I don't let him pick me up in the first place—I like soft soap, a flannel and a duck for my bath. My idea of an agreeable man is one who agrees with me. Nor do I like a man who boasts of his conquests. If he's keeping open bed for half London, what's in it for me?

As he is leaving, Superman moves into action:

"We must meet again sometime." (Smouldering glance.)

"We must."

"Where can I get hold of you?"

"Wherever you like, darling." (Smouldering glance.)

"No, I meant your telephone number. We must have dinner sometime." (Lunch if either of you is married.)

Superman then memorises the number until he gets

outside the room, when he writes it down. Sexual Norm overhears and jots it down in his diary, alongside the addresses of hundreds of other girls he's never had the courage to telephone. In fact, knowing he's got her number and could ring her up lessens his desire to try.

THE DATE

"And afterwards, Miss Dyson, you might like to come round to my place . . ."

My experience has been that men who are interested ring you up within twenty-four hours, and ask you out.

I get very irritated when they telephone and say: Guess who. I always guess wrong deliberately. Nor do I like men who ring up at twelve o'clock and say how about lunch today, giving you no time to wash your hair or appear faintly unavailable. Or, when you don't want to speak to them, give someone else's name, Omar Shariff or Sean Connery, to get you to the telephone. Even more maddening is when they call you and keep you on slow burn by chatting you up for a quarter of an hour and then don't ask you out.

I don't like it either when men, having got your address, drop in uninvited at all hours of the night expecting an ecstatic welcome just when you've gone to bed covered in cold cream and rollers. This is a fundamental would-be-seducer's error. Nothing makes a woman less sexually receptive than feeling unattractive.

For the first date, any man who's worth his salt will spend a bomb on dinner, the theatre, etc. Equally, the girl who is worth his assault will spend a bomb on a new dress, shoes, make-up, and at the hairdresser's. Sex is expensive.

Most courtships seem to be carried on in restaurants, helped along by soft lights and hard liquor.

Superman never takes a girl on public transport—the lighting's so frightful. It's either cars, taxis, or a short walk (and I mean short), if it's not raining or freezing, under the stars.

ON THE FIRST DATE, MOST MEN TAKE YOU TO A RESTAURANT.

Superman gives you plenty to drink, doesn't translate the menu from French for you, or spend so much time chatting up the *patron* and asking the waiters about their mothers that he's got no time for you.

"Darling, I'm so hungry I could eat you."

He also arranges for you to sit side by side on a bench seat at a decent distance from other people so that he can brush your hand with his occasionally, or even put a hand on your thigh when he's making a telling point.

"I definitely think Arsenal" (playful pummel) "are going to win the cup."

On a bench seat too, it's much easier to make eyes at other people if you get bored.

If you sit at a table opposite a man, you miss half his sweet nothings, you've got nowhere to look if there's a lapse in the conversation, and you're quite likely to waste the whole meal playing footy footy with a table leg.

Another point to remember is that if your dinner-date chooses what he's going to eat with infinite care, then eats all three courses, he's not really keen on you. It's those untouched plates of food that indicate a grand passion.

Meanness of course is a great turn-off. Those men who say: "I thoroughly recommend the grape-fruit, they sugar it awfully well here, and why not have pasta for a main course?" afterwards expect you to pay for your dinner horizontally. The same type always fails to conceal that he's keeping the bill afterwards, and if he takes you to a party first, encourages you to fill up on the canapés so you'll only need a very plain omelette later.

Lunch I have always thought is an even more erotic start to an affaire than dinner. When you have the enforced discipline of getting back to the office or the children, you always come on much stronger than you would normally.

OR YOU CAN TAKE HER TO A PUB.

Sexual Norm usually takes girls to his pub on the first date, because it's cheap, because his friends will be impressed if they see him with a girl, because there's someone else to talk to if he runs out of conversation. And he knows where the Gents is.

I'm not wild about pubs, they're all right in their place but not for courting, with all those bursts of well lubricated laughter, and large men in sports coats wanting to break into song. The bar stools are just the wrong length for my legs, and if you collar a table someone always comes shuffling over clutching a glass of lager and a cheese roll, sits down and inhibits your conversation.

Invariably too your date drinks pints of beer, when you have a gin and tonic, and as you finish long before he does, if you're polite you hide your glass, or if you're like me, you rattle your ice or ostentatiously eat your lemon peel to encourage him to buy you another.

Pubs however are infinitely sexier than Indian restaurants: nothing could be less turning on than flocked wallpaper, bright lights, glasses of warm light ale, a meat vindaloo-flavoured kiss afterwards, and onions, which recur through the night.

Going to the theatre is nice for a first date—as long as you choose something jolly and the man doesn't spend the whole time grumbling that there's nowhere to put his legs. You should also dine afterwards rather than before.

Cinemas are all right too—but here again you should dine afterwards with plenty of alcohol. There's always something faintly depressing about the return to reality: your date doesn't look quite as good as Steve McQueen, and you certainly don't look so good as Jane Fonda. Horror films are excellent because they're good for a giggle, and you've got a marvellous excuse for pretending to be frightened and clutching each other.

THE PASS

Sexual Norm by this time will be treading out the ground for the pass. We all know the tell-tale signs: the slowing down of a car on a lonely road, the hand edging along the back seat, the manoeuvring into an empty office in the lunch hour, the sidling up on the faded rose-patterned sofa accompanied by a murmur of: "Are your flat mates really out?"

The girl if she fancies the man is wondering how much and how soon she can give in without feeling cheap.

Norm has been known to pounce from the arm of a girl's chair, and be rudely deposited on the floor when she leaps to her feet.

A lot of men reluctant to face a rebuff, make verbal passes.

"Can I come up for coffee?"

"Does your husband ever go away?"

"When are you next going up to London?" (This to a country wife.)

"I thought next time we lunched it might be fun if we had a leg of chicken and white wine at my flat."

"The grass really isn't wet, you know."

"Our bodies do talk the same language, don't they?" (This one usually on the dance floor.)

Or the more direct but less subtle approach: "I fantastically want to fuck you."

Sexual Norm, who realises the importance of being a good sexual conversationalist, sometimes says: "Would you mind awfully if I kissed you, Jennifer?" and then lunges even if she says no.

It must be difficult being a man. If you pounce too soon everyone calls you a wolf, if you hold off too long everyone calls you a queer. If you make a pass of Khyber-like proportions at a girl who fancies you, she'll say you're wonderfully passionate, if you do exactly the same to a girl who doesn't, she'll complain you're mauling her.

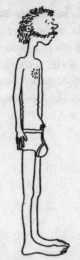

"Big feet, darling . . .?"

In theory, Superman is never in a hurry. His timing is so good that he always waits to make a pass at you at exactly the moment you're worrying he might not—so you plummet like the proverbial ripe plum into his arms.

But the whole pass-making business has become such a game—the man waiting until you're getting worried, you falling over backwards not to appear worried—that it all goes on until you both go off the boil.

Other men are so impervious to the come-on signs that you don't know if they're genuinely shy or just playing hard to get. They're so reserved you wonder if someone else has reserved them already.

The smooth operator of course, who always prefers to

play on home ground, lures you back to his flat. Soon you're lying on his sofa without your shoes. The central heating is up, the lights are dimmed, soft music is spilling into the room, and out of the corner of your eye in the next room you can see the most enormous double bed covered in furs. Within minutes the zips are down.

* * * * *

Bed

> *"Sex isn't the best thing in the world, or the worst thing in the world, but there's nothing else quite like it."*
>
> W. C. FIELDS.

LOCATION

Once a man knows a girl's interested, where does he take her? It's all right if both of them have got a flat—but if they haven't there's all the hassell of packing a suitcase to spend a few hours at a hotel, or borrowing a friend's flat to 'change in', or waiting till nightfall to do it in the back of a car, or for summer to do it in the long grass.

Wives always say they couldn't possibly commit adultery in their own house, but lust is a great leveller.

Superman books a room at the Ritz and launches the girl into a sea of vice with a bottle of champagne, ordering smoked salmon in the interval. He believes in mixing pleasure with pleasure.

I've often wondered why smoked salmon is so erotic. Perhaps because it reminds one of rather warm bare flesh.

Before he was married Sexual Norm used to commit fawnication (sic) on a creaking single bed. The girl invariably bumped into the landlady on her way to the bathroom on the next floor.

Some women with marvellous figures like to be undressed before they leap into bed. And for this reason boys ought to take a course in undoing bras at prep-school. But with most people it's a race to get undressed

"But Angus, I always thought one never *wore anything underneath . . ."*

and into bed before the other person has time to see their stretch marks or spindly calves.

Bachelors sometimes take their clothes off and fold them up in polythene bags. Older hippies get undressed in another room, so they can remove their corsets in private and return with a swish of terry towelling.

Adulterers look in the cupboard or under the bed. Superman takes the telephone off the hook. He also has a fire extinguisher on the wall in case the girl bursts into flames.

Once in bed both parties breathe deeply and say "A-a-a-ah" several times. This is usually construed as ecstasy, but is in reality because of the coldness of the sheets and other people's hands.

People always try harder with new people. Sexual Norm will spend the next ten minutes worrying whether he's giving the girl enough sexual foreplay or fiveplay, and then grimly thinking about cricket or football to keep his mind off sex. He occasionally says '*Howzat*'.

The girl, remembering what the sex books told her about not lying back and being passive, will be frenziedly stroking Norm's neck, tickling his toes, kissing his navel, and putting on such a display of acrobatics that he has to try and think even harder about cricket or football.

Finally with the words 'there are no frigid women, only incompetent men' ringing in his ears, Norm starts threshing away like a sewing machine that's got out of hand.

THE BLAND LEADING THE BLAND

Then come the lies.

The man, crossing his fingers, will say: "I don't do this very often, you know."

The girl, crossing her legs, will say: "Neither do I."

He: "I've only been to bed with, er, five women in my life."

She (uncrossing her legs): "This is the first affaire I've had since I've been married."

He: "I wouldn't dream of going to bed with a girl I didn't feel deeply about." (Feeling deeply under her dress.)

Several asterisks later he will say: "That was wonderful, darling. Was it wonderful for you, darling?"

*"Gosh, that was marvellous, darling.
Was it wonderful for you, darling?"*

I'm sure one of the reasons for the permissive society is because girls wear so few underclothes these days and are more getatable. Whenever I went out with a new man—fifteen years ago—I used to buy a new pantie-girdle to keep my curves at bay, which acted as a complete chastity belt. And, even worse, there were those all-in-one corselettes, which totally denied access.

MULTIPLE BOREGASM

Sex books in fact have made Sex absolutely impossible. Havealot Ellis and the still small voice of Kama Sutra were all right, but recently I was sent a book consisting of 287 pages devoted to Oragenitalism, which needed a degree in engineering to be understood. And you can go crazy trying to memorise all the refinements of *The Sensuous Woman*. "The Velvet Buzz Saw, the Butterfly Flick." Nor can I see that it honestly adds anything to your sex life if you suddenly disappear in the middle of a steaming session to get chocolate ice-cream from the fridge to smear all over each other. And think of the laundry bills.

I'm sure all those ludicrously controlled positions they advocate are responsible for the high incidence of slipped discs these days. I wouldn't be surprised if most sex books were written by osteopaths to encourage business.

"Oh damn, I've lost the place again."

Cosmopolitan magazine the other day was exhorting girls to excite and cajole their lovers with wildly obscene language. Sexual Norm, who's been brought up not to swear in front of a lady, would be absolutely horrified.

In fact after reading a sex book manual, I'm amazed any man dares pounce on a girl at all. He must be so worried about 'ejaculatory incompetence' or being a tower of jelly in a crisis, or not being able to come ten times a night. Then there's always the problem of having wined not wisely but too well. Of the four stages of drunkenness: jocose, bellicose, lachrymose and comatose, it is essential to catch the girl at the post-jocose stage.

And novels are so sexy too these days that even if a couple are having a quiet read before going to bed, the girl is liable to become insanely amorous just after the man's taken his sleeping pills.

LUST IS THE MOTHER OF INVENTION

I'm a believer in lust—if two people fancy each other silly, they usually have a nice time in bed without the aid of chocolate ice-cream or the Velvet Buzz Saw.

Of course there will be men like the Old Man of Thermopylae who never did anyone properly, or lazy men, who believe in labour saving vices, and just lie on their backs and let the girl do all their work.

But on the whole I think the good lover has a way with women as some people do with horses—he makes them relax, he creates the kind of cosy emotional atmosphere in which a woman is not afraid to ask him to do the thing he wants to her. He is also an enthusiast, he cares for making a woman happy rather than making her, he is not frightened of getting his feet or anything else wet—relief would be just a lovely wallow away.

I don't think most women are crazy about sexual athletes. If he can twist you into every position in the Kama Sutra that's gym not sex. Nor are they wild about marathons. The third day he rose from the bed may be all right for some, but it's no good if he doesn't press the right buttons.

Finally the most important thing in a good lover is a sense of humour. He should be someone who can send the whole thing sky high, who wouldn't mind if you were having an off day or didn't feel up to it.

"But sweetest, why in the bedroom?"

BATHS

Afterwards lovers are supposed to have baths together, which I've always thought was an overrated pastime, particularly if you sit at the wrong end and have the taps digging into your back, with one side scalded and the other one frozen. On the other hand if you don't have a bath together, whoever has last bath not only has to make the bed but also clean the bath.

THE VENERABLE BIDET

Then of course there's the bidet—somehow if you go to someone's house and see a bidet in their bathroom you assume they must be sexually switched on, or French.

Sexual Norm thinks bidets are for bathing the dog. American girl in Paris hotel: "Dig that crazy drinking fountain."

VASECTOMY

According to a recent article this is the most beautiful thing a man can do for a woman; it's also one of the shrewdest. If a man has a vasectomy, he can have an absolute hayride sleeping with anyone he wants to without danger. His wife however is completely stymied if she suddenly gets pregnant.

DIRTY WEEKENDS

"But, darling, when you said a dirty weekend . . ."

Dirty weekends are divided into two kinds, the first when both the man and the woman intend to sleep with each other, the second when the man is intending to sleep with the woman.

As the former usually take place in hotels, the couple's main problem is to appear married, because if the hotel staff rumble the fact that they are not married they may easily try to put one of them in the Annex. A girl friend of mine recently spent a dirty weekend in Scotland, punctuated by dour Highland Ladies banging on the bedroom door and crying: "Come out, come out."

"Oh for goodness sake, Annabel, we've got to leave early in the morning."

The couple should therefore remember not to roll up in separate cars with separate luggage bearing different names. They should also not appear too animated at mealtimes, but gaze gloomily into space like other married couples. The girl should also remember not to ask the man whether he likes sugar in his coffee at breakfast or what name she should put in the register.

One wife I know after her husband had spent a dirty weekend in the Cotswolds with his secretary found the bill in his name. When taxed, the husband told her it was his partner's bill. "The swine always uses my name when he gets up to any of his tricks." The wife believed him, and went round saying what a louse her husband's partner was.

If a girl goes on one of the latter dirty weekends when the man is trying to make her and has promised there are no strings attached, he usually invites her to stay with married friends who immediately steer her into a room with a large double bed, which they claim is their only spare room. Or he will take her on a boat, and not until it's at sea, does she realise it only sleeps one.

Love

LOVE

"*If you believe in me, I'll believe in you*"

ALICE IN WONDERLAND.

"*I am melancholy when thou art absent, look like an ass when thou art present, wake for thee when I should be asleep, and even dream of thee, when I am awake; sigh much, drink little, eat less, court solitude, am grown very entertaining to my self, and (as I am informed) very troublesome to everybody else. If this be not love, it is madness, and then it is pardonable.*" The Old Bachelor.

A great deal of time is spent kidding oneself a man is keen on one when he isn't. Once a man is hooked he will:

find every one of your idiosyncrasies endearing

roar with laughter at your most inane jokes. (People in love sound like hyenas)

write you letters, when he's going to see you the next day, which he tears up

bore all his friends talking about you in the tones of gross hyperbole

lose interest in everyone else

telephone all the time

make heroic efforts to spend every moment he possibly can with you to the extent of driving you 30 miles home after a date, picking you up from the office to take you to the station, or crossing London in the rush hour for the sake of being with you for two minutes.

Men quite often behave like this to a girl before they get her into bed. If they act like this afterwards, she's on to a good thing and should stay on.

NORMAN'S SEXUAL CONQUEST

Being susceptible, Norm falls in love about three times a year. At present he is hooked on a well stacked typist in the office called Dental Floss.

His wife Honor can always detect the signs. She hears Norm yelling for clean underpants in the morning. She then watches him putting deodorant between his toes, cutting himself shaving because his hand is shaking with excitement, shrieking with agony when his new French Aftershave gets into the cuts, leaving a snowfall of talcum powder on the bathroom floor, and cutting his toe nails surreptitiously into the waste-paper basket instead of in bed as usual.

He then polishes his shoes, changes his mind five times about what tie he's going to wear, picks the only rose in the garden for his buttonhole, spends hours combing his hair over his bald patch, and can be seen slipping a toothbrush into his briefcase. Sometimes he cleans his teeth.

Honor notices he has also taken to carrying cigarettes and a lighter although he doesn't smoke, and spending a lot of evenings at regimental dinners or out with the boys and returning completely sober. When she rides in the car she finds her seat belt has been let out to accommodate a vast bust.

FOR EVER AMBER

Some men are so filled with caution, they can never bring themselves to propose. I've seen so many girls go out for years with a man in the hope that they might hook him in the end. They spend their time looking for signs: "He's talked about our going on holiday together, he's going to get a house when the lease of his flat runs out, he's taken me to meet his mother, he's got my photograph in his wallet, I've looked in his diary and he's got nothing but squash with Geoffrey and cricket fixtures for the next six months." But the man still won't say he loves her or ask her to marry him.

The girl becomes more and more bitchy and resentful, even though she knows she's not furthering her cause. Men like to come home to someone restful and neutral who doesn't make scenes.

Or she resorts to the awful boredom of playing games, flirting with other men to keep her man on his toes, or rather on his elbows.

If only she had the courage to break it off. But it's rather like trying to get out of a tepid bath, the water is getting colder and colder, but it's still warmer than the cold outside.

Some girls try and shove a man Gretna Green-wards by showing him what a grand little home-maker she is, mucking out his flat, washing his shirts and rugger shorts, being fantastically good with all his married friends' children, currying favour and chicken leftovers. But I don't think it works.

"Well, I just thought we could go out after all . . ."

I'm against Women's Lib because I think women come unstuck when they do the chasing. They can't keep the beseeching or the stammer out of their voices when they ring men up. Then there is the expense of giving a whole cocktail party, in order to extend a casual invitation to one man, who probably doesn't come anyway, or asking a man to dinner and filling the place with so many flowers and candles it looks like a funeral parlour.

Now most young men are far more house proud and domesticated than girls. They live in bachelor flats with all mod cons. They shop at the late-night supermarket, and their washing is done for them by the dragon in the launderette who has a soft spot for men. Their shirts drip dry over the bath. They have no difficulty in getting a char.

In the kitchen in the evening they know all about basil and tarragon as they whisk around in their butcher-boy aprons, blinding you with domestic science. They are even marvellous at washing up. Gone are the good old days, when indulgent wives used to say: "Norm's a wonderfully imaginative cook, but it takes me three days to clear up the pots and pans after him."

As they listen to the Women's Lib screeching, men must wonder why they should bother to marry at all, and get terrible complexes about enslaving a suffering female, or turning a graduate into a cabbage. They don't need wives to darn their socks or the holes in their arguments.

THE COOLING-OFF PERIOD

Nothing is sadder than to feel a man going off, it's like trying to hold water in cupped hands.

The coward usually does it with a kiss, and then stops ringing up. If he starts saying things like: "I'm awfully *fond* of you, Jennifer," or "I love you but I'm not *in* love with you," or "We don't have much in common except the obvious thing, do we?" Or if he's married: "I think Honor suspects something, so perhaps we'd better cool it for a month or two"—you know the end is very near.

Personal Habits

HYGIENE—ME AND MY FIVE O'CLOCK SHADOW

"Well, it's quicker than a bath any day."

Television advertising has made us positively paranoiac about hygiene. A man hardly looks at a girl without fretting whether he's forgotten to use his roll-on deodorant, his anti-perspirant, his Lifebuoy Soap, or his

Gold Spot. A lot of his time will be spent shaving twice a day so he can dunk himself in aftershave, cleaning his teeth, worrying about the Y-fronts and Wherefores of Under Stains, and lobbying to have a bidet installed in the office Gents.

The sweet smell of success has been replaced by the success of sweet smell. If a man smells remotely rancid you can assume he hasn't got a television, or only watches B.B.C.

I like men to wear scent. I hate mouths like mossy caverns and I prefer fur coats to furlined nostrils. But it is very turning off if a man stops his car and starts crunching Polos, before he crushes you in his arms and fills your mouth with peppermint-flavoured splinters.

The nicest men taste faintly of garlic—but not of onions.

Sexual Norm, who wants to get his teeth into Dental Floss, is wondering whether he ought to get circumcised because he's heard it's more hygienic.

CLOTHES

Once upon a time there were hard and fast rules about what a gentleman wore. But recently the young have raised two fingers at fashion, and now anything goes as long as you wear it without selfconsciousness, and with style.

One was always being told that no gentleman would wear rings on anything but his little finger, or coats with belts, or suits without a tie or braces—but somehow with shoulder-length hair they all look perfectly all right.

I'm still not wild about jerkins, or knickerbockers, or any kind of hats, baggy flannel trousers, lovat-green cardigans or white polo-necked sweaters on older men trying to look younger ("a touch of white is so flattering near the face when you get beyond a certain age").

I'm also allergic to shorts except on athletes, belted camel-hair coats, vests, and gloves except on ski instructors or gynaecologists. And I can do without the anorak brigade, and old school ties—that awful idea of looking at someone's neck first to see if he's acceptable.

It also amazes me how few men have a sense of colour.

"Your HAT, Charles."

They don't seem to realise that grey looks hell with a sallow skin, and red with an English red-brick complexion.

Or, as a chum of mine said who went to see a friend in prison: "Brown simply isn't Gordon's colour."

Well dressed men always seem to get someone else to wear their suits in for them. Sexual Norm wears a blazer with a Rotary Club badge, a club tie with shields on it, and a battery of fountain pens in his breast pocket which leak onto his white nylon shirt when he presses himself against girls.

HAIR

Very few Englishmen seem to realise the importance of having their hair cut properly.

They also seem to have no control over their barbers.

"But, Celia, I'm working until 3 every morning. How do you expect me to get it cut?"

Having just grown their hair to a reasonable length over their collars, they suddenly start muttering about having too many wisps round their ears or the older men in the office looking disapproving, and disappear to their barbers. They emerge with their sideboards shaven, absolutely non-existent back, front and sides, and looking just about as gruesomely sexless as soldiers used to on their first leave from National Service.

It takes at least two months for them to be bearable to look at again.

I can't think why they're so reluctant to grow their hair. Not only is long hair pretty, it also covers a multitude of sins, such as an ugly hair line, a dirty neck, protuberant or dirty ears, and carbuncles.

Dreadfully square men who fancy themselves often have it cut short at the back but slightly longer at the front, so that it curls on their foreheads and makes them look boyish.

BEARDS

I'm not wild about beards on men or women, particularly if the men have very full red lips, or their beards are always getting clogged with soup, cream or melted butter. I suppose if you shut your eyes you can fancy you're being kissed by some furry animal who might be Jupiter in disguise.

The Common Market

THE COMMON MARKET

In the next few years, the country will be flooded with foreigners, Frenchmen who would a-wooing go, Italians who take every remark you make with a pinch of flesh.

Wives will greet their husbands with the question: "Had a good Dago at the office, darling?"

When I was eighteen I spent a fortnight in Majorca with a girl friend. The beauty of the Majorcan men affected us like a fever and they soon returned the compliment. The first day we sat on the beach we suddenly became aware of hundreds of small, dark, handsome men edging inch by inch towards us on their stomachs like an army on manoeuvres, and soon we were surrounded. Every night we seemed to go out with at least six men.

After a few days my friend settled for a flamenco dancer, but I couldn't make up my mind between a taxi driver and a telephone mechanic called Angel, until one evening the taxi driver took me for a long walk along the beach. A huge white moon had turned the sea to gunmetal.

The taxi driver removed his coat and hung it on a breakwater, then took my scarf and spread it out on the sand. How like Sir Walter Raleigh, I thought, very moved, and was preparing to sit on it when I was firmly pushed out of the way and he sat on it himself. He was damned if he was going to have his new suit covered in sand. After that I settled for Angel.

What other single men is a girl likely to get off with on holiday? Sexual athletes from the Gorbals in their prehistoric shorts and their sandals and socks. Pallid Belgians in snorkel masks, airtubes and flippers looking like something out of Doctor Who. Germans who spring 100 yards across a crowded beach to light your cigarette. Danes so impossibly blue-eyed and beautiful that they couldn't be interested in women at all.

Beware too the French gigolo with his curls and flat stomach, his flashy crawl and his superb English. If you spill Ambre Solaire on his shirt, he'll drop his accent in a trice and turn out to be some hairdresser from Palmers Green.

Even the stolid English wolf will find his sheep's clothing too hot on holidays and emerge in his full colours as Playboy of the Western World.

When he gazes deep into your eyes and murmurs: "Let's spend the rest of our lives together like that ah, um, you know, that classical couple who spent their lives together" he doesn't mean it. Holidays produce beautiful ephemeral relationships but rarely husbands.

Angel the telephone mechanic turned up in England that winter. Without his suntan, without a job, but with gold teeth and a shiny suit, and speaking no English, he was a far less attractive proposition.

When Sexual Norman goes on holiday he gets drunk on the B.E.A. flight going out and sings 'Valencia here I come'.

Man and his Recreations

MAN AND HIS RECREATIONS

"I'd rather he had his hobbies than other women."

I think a lot of male-female resentment stems from men spending so much time away from their beloveds— not even earning money, but spending it instead in clubs, pubs, or playing games.

THE CLUB

One of the last bastions of male chauvinism. Not only do they discriminate against women but also against each other. If you are Jewish or foreign and want to get into one of the more august clubs, you have to change your name not once but twice in case they ask you what your name was before you changed it.

If a wife rings up to speak to her husband, the call is taken by the porter or the steward who puts his hand over the receiver and asks: "Are you in, my Lord?"

After lunch at a boys' school, dining in one of the ladies' annexes is about the most unglamorous thing in the world. Awful décor, overhead lighting, cress on everything and musty waitresses called Dolly with indiscreetly dyed hair. The ladies usually consist of a few felt hats, and their pale daughters fingering their pearls and about to go back to school.

HIS FRIENDS

"Darling, you must meet Leo and Roger, my oldest friends."

"Some of my best friends are friends."

One of a man's most irritating habits, along with revving up his car when he thinks you ought to be ready, leaving one sock in his trousers and talking about time and motion when he watches you doing housework, is showing off in front of his friends. He only has to be surrounded by a few cronies to start making snide remarks, about you but more likely about your friends. If you take him to task at the time, you will be accused of making a scene. If you bring it up later, he will have forgotten what he said, and accuse you of making a mountain out of a molehill.

One of the silliest things one is ever told as a gel, is to avoid men who haven't got any men friends.

77

"Yes, definitely a big end ..."

Cars are a complete sex substitute. Why else do men refer to the beastly things as 'she'? Let a carman into your life, and you will be woken every morning by the squeak of chamois leather, or be stood up on a date because he's 'moving cars' this weekend. Carmen howl round the shopping centre effing and blinding at every traffic light, wear awful gloves with holes in the back, rush up to anything with a strap round its bonnet and pat it as though it had just won the Grand National, and are so used to lying underneath cars that they always take the underneath position when making love to you, and then complain your big end's gone. Beforehand they wind you up with a starting handle.

On the coldest day in winter, they put woolly hats with pom-poms on, and drive you for hours with the hood down to blow the cobwebs and your wig and everything else away.

In the summer as a treat they'll take you to Silverstone where you will stand pressed against a railing surrounded by men in flat caps talking about gaskets. Occasionally a car flashes by making the sort of noise that unpleasantly resembles a dentist's drill, and a voice says "that was Old Graham", or Jackie. If you say you admire a certain driver, it's always someone who, it turns out, kicked the bucket last week.

A few years ago, sports cars were the thing, but now I'm glad to see they have been replaced by Rolls-Royces with blacked-out windows. Riding in them you always think the weather is much worse than it is, and feel very cheerful when you get out.

BOATS ARE EVEN WORSE

Sailing is absolutely terrifying. You arrive for the weekend all dressed up in brand-new old clothes with your hair just done, and as soon as you set sail a dirty great wave rolls up and absolutely drenches you. Next moment, the sail is lying on the water, and the darling amiable man who asked you on the boat has turned into Captain Bligh and is yelling blue murder at you. Something about going aft. The nicest men become absolute monsters once they get a bit of string between their hands. Most of your weekend will be spent in the hold, cooking meals which everyone throws up.

The amazing thing about sailing is that although by day the men bellow at you and can't tell the girls from the buoys, at night everything changes. The boat is moored, the whisky comes out and they're all ready to seek out your Jolly Erogenous zones and play deck coitus. If there is another couple aboard, you are bound to have changed partners before the weekend is out, for there is something about lack of space, appallingly uncomfortable beds, and seasickness, that makes people incredibly randy.

GOLF

If you go out with a man who plays golf, your biggest problem will be not to laugh the first time you see him in action. Once they get on the course, the most sober, steadfast and demure individuals suddenly blossom out like court jesters, in the most brilliant colours and fashions—lemon-yellow caps, pale-blue anoraks, cherry-pink trousers. And when they wiggle their feet to get their stance right they look exactly like cats preparing to pee.

Their language is even more colourful. My uncle had a house near the fourth tee in Yorkshire, and all his children had to wear ear plugs.

In the club house afterwards they will suddenly start kissing your hand, downing gins and tons, asking you what's your poison and saying haw, haw, haw all the time.

Golfers never have one night stands—they hole in one.

RUGGER MEN

Here comes Thunderthighs.

Rugger can be the most romantic game in the world—

who could resist Gareth Edwards? It can also be the most boring, if you're watching on the touchline in the icy cold and it's Harlequins 42, H.A.C. nil.

After the game, having covered themselves with mud and glory, rugger players spend hours and hours in the bath, and then expect you to talk to other rugger wives while they down pint after pint of beer. Occasionally in the back of a car, they will make a forward pass at you.

If you marry a rugger player, you won't get sex on Friday night in case you put his eye out, all the towels will disappear, and by the end of the season his suitcase of kit no longer needs carrying, it walks by itself.

Rugger players love orgies, because they remind them of the scrum.

"But Gilbert, I played front row last night . . ."

ROWING MEN
Row me oh, oh Row me oh.

HORSEY MEN
Goodness, she isn't wearing a bridle.

Horses and sex seem to go together. If you've got something between your legs all day, you want to carry on in the same vein at night.

Horsey men have tough faces, vice-like thigh muscles (although that may be an illusion created by their jodhpurs), and figures of eight engraved on their bottoms from sitting on so many shooting sticks.

They will tighten your girths before they mount you and pin a red rosette on you afterwards. Never make love to them upside down or the luck will run out of them.

SHOOTING

Hearing about shooting is very tedious, with all those Harris Tweedledumbs who roll up at a girl's flat with a bloody grouse in each hand and proceed to twelve-bore everything but the pants off her, telling her about their exploits on the Glorious Twelfth. Going shooting on the other hand is rather fun—like walking under armed escort—as long as you make sure the guns stop for a long boozey lunch in the middle of the day.

Between each drive you will hear rather ambiguous cries:

"Where's Rufus?"

"Picking up birds in the woods."

or

"Hey, that's my cock you've got hold of."

The guns work off so much aggression being beastly to their dogs that they're usually quite nice to women.

BRIDGE

Definitely addictive—people who are short on conversation or old before their time play bridge—and once hooked they would rather play than take a girl out. All bridge players sweat heavily.

FOOTBALL

I've never actually met a football player but 'Match of the Day' is an absolute godsend. It's the only time you will have free to wash your hair, or pluck your eyebrows —your man will be absolutely glued to the box. Watch out for Action Replays, though.

Orgies

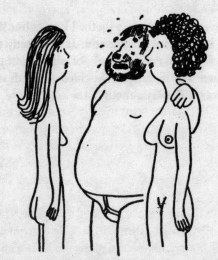

"Er yes, yes, Miss Weldon, the matter of your overdraft will be quite *all right . . ."*

Two way mirror on the wall, who is the barest of us all?

Very few people will admit they've been to an orgy, and those who do say they only watched and it was very boring.

"No central heating, and not enough to drink," said a male friend of mine. "And lots of bank managers in their underpants talking about cars. It was rather like having a bath with one's Nanny. Not much fun and nowhere to look."

This is a far cry from one's fantasies of pulsating wall-to-wall couples, people in sheets drinking wine out of goatskins, girls coming out of pies and crushing black grapes with very white teeth, and sophisticates with jaded parrots watching through two-way mirrors.

I'd be a dead loss at an orgy, for I'd be convinced everyone in the room was looking at my awful feet. In order to participate I'd have to drink myself silly, and as soon as I drink myself silly I feel sick and am a write-off sexually.

But I'm fascinated by the ethics of orgies. Do men come up to girls they want to couple with, tap them on the shoulder, and say shall we lie this one out? And to get everyone going, do they say: last man in works the gramophone? And do they have Ladies Excuse Mes? How awful too if no one asked you and you were a floor flower all evening.

If Superman goes to an orgy, of course, it's like the first day of the sales, with all the women trying to get at him. Sexual Norm however, although he is excited about loving dangerously, is worried about his wallet and the size of his member, and is still in his Y-fronts. He tries to look like a film producer, hoping that the starlet in the corner might be the sort who wants to get to the top on her back.

Dental Floss, who is looking skittish in Woolworths pearls, exhorts him to strip.

"You've got nothing to hide," she says.

"That's what I'm afraid of," says Norm. He watches her rush up to a trio of car salesmen.

"You three can have a body like mine," she cries.

Norm looks across at his wife Honor, who is still wearing her roll-on and talking about deepfreezes to another housewife. Norm decides he's really much better doing it with Honor. He wishes he was completely hairy up to his waist like a satyr, then it wouldn't show if he took his underpants off. It must have been easy for satyrs in the old days. He wishes he could go home.

Next day however he will regale his friends in the pub with a torrid account of the mountains of heaving flesh, adding: "I really didn't know where to put myself."

"Come again?"